Rebecca powers

FACTS AT YOUR FINGERTIPS

WEATHER

DAVID MARSHALL

SIMON & SCHUSTER
YOUNG BOOKS

This book was prepared for
Simon & Schuster Young Books
by Globe Enterprises, Nantwich, Cheshire

Design and artwork: SPL Design
Photographs: ZEFA except
Allsport (5, 25tr), Science Photo Library (24, 25l, 25br, 29),
Rupert Horrox (front cover left)
Typesetting and layout: Quark Xpress

First published in Great Britain in 1993
by Simon & Schuster Young Books

Simon & Schuster Young Books
Campus 400, Maylands Avenue
Hemel Hempstead, Herts HP2 7EZ

Printed and bound in Belgium
by Proost International Book Production

A catalogue record for this book
is available from the British Library
ISBN 0 7500 1297 8

CONTENTS

4

WHAT IS THE

WEATHER?

Will it be fine today? Will it rain? Much of what we do is affected by the weather and we often have to change our plans because the weather is not suitable. ▶

◀ The weather affects our clothes, our houses and the kind of crops that farmers grow. Too much rain means that the ground will flood, too little and there is a drought.

The effects of the weather can be a matter of life and death. Fierce storms can wreck ships, destroy whole towns and devastate communities. By studying weather patterns, we can warn people when to prepare for bad weather. ▶

ATMOSPHERE

The layers of gases that surround the Earth are known as the atmosphere. They stretch up to about 1,000 km above our heads. If they were not there, nothing could live on Earth as it would be burning hot during the day and icy cold at night.

Heat from the sun stirs up the atmosphere and keeps it moving. Weather is really just the movement of air around the planet. Sometimes the air is still and hot—sometimes windy and cold. Sometimes it is full of water—other times it can be stirred into a raging, swirling hurricane.

The atmosphere has several layers all of which are different from each other. The lowest layer is called the troposphere. Here is the air that we breathe and the place where all our weather happens. ➤

AIR PRESSURE

The pressure of the air around us changes all time. The sun heats the ground making the gases close to it expand. Areas where the gas is thin, have a lower pressure than areas of denser gas. Whenever the air pressure is different between two places on Earth, the wind tries to even things up by blowing from the high pressure area to the low pressure area.

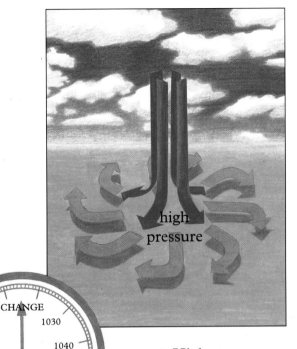
high pressure

▲ Air pressure is measured in millibars on an instrument known as barometer.

▲ High pressure occurs when cool air falls towards the ground. The air spirals out at the bottom giving fine weather. It spirals clockwise in the northern hemisphere and anticlockwise south of the equator.

low pressure

◄ Low pressure occurs when warm air rises. Air is sucked into a low pressure area causing winds which spiral clockwise in the southern hemisphere and anticlockwise in the northern. Low pressure brings rain.

RADIATION

The sun gives out a huge amount of energy and light, only a small part of which reaches the Earth. The atmosphere scatters much of this energy making the sky blue and protecting us from harmful rays. Energy that reaches the ground is absorbed and given out as heat. The amount of heat that the Earth loses and gains all the time is about the same and so the temperature in each part of the world remains more or less even.

▲ Dark and dull surfaces like buildings and forests absorb more of the sun's energy than white, bright surfaces like snow and ice.

Because the Earth is round, energy from the sun falling at the equator spreads over less ground than energy falling at the poles. This means the ground heats up more at the equator than at the poles. ►

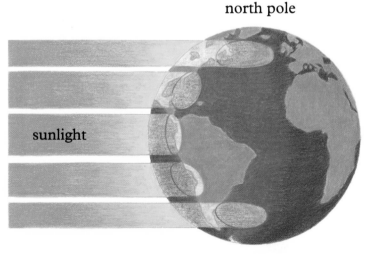

north pole

sunlight

equator

south pole

WATER IN THE AIR

Water exists in the atmosphere in one of three ways: water vapour which is an invisible gas; water droplets; or ice crystals. There is a limit to the amount of water vapour that air can hold. When it cannot hold any more, the air is saturated and the extra vapour condenses as drops of water. Warm air can hold far more water vapour than cold air. When the air is really warm and moist, it feels sticky and we say that it is humid.

▲ When the sun comes out after a rainstorm, water drops on trees and plants disappear. This is because they evaporate into the air as water vapour.

◄ Warm, damp air forms ice patterns on window glass when the temperature outside is freezing. The air next to the window cools and can no longer hold as much water vapour. This condenses on the glass and forms ice crystals.

THE WATER CYCLE

There is only a certain amount of water in the world—it is constantly going round in a huge circle. This water cycle provides the Earth with a continuous supply of fresh water.

▲ Clouds cool as they rise and can no longer hold as much water. Rain or snow fall the Earth.

The sun dries the soil on the land and takes water from the leaves of plants and trees into the air.▶

◀Rainwater collects in streams and rivers flowing down to the sea.

▼As the sun heats the seas, rivers and lakes, water evaporates and is carried into the sky where it condenses and forms clouds.

CLOUDS

Clouds appear when water vapour in the air cools down forming tiny droplets of water or ice. There are three main types of cloud—cirrus, which are made from tiny ice crystals, stratus, which are light-grey blankets of cloud and cumulus, large fluffy clouds that usually mean fine weather. If the uprush of air that forms cumulus cloud is violent then the cloud turns black and gives thunder, lightning and rain.

▲ Very high, wispy cirrus clouds can mean unsettled weather is on the way.

Clusters of cumulus clouds show that the weather will stay fine. ▼

Low lying, black nimbostratus clouds mean heavy snow or rain is imminent. ▼

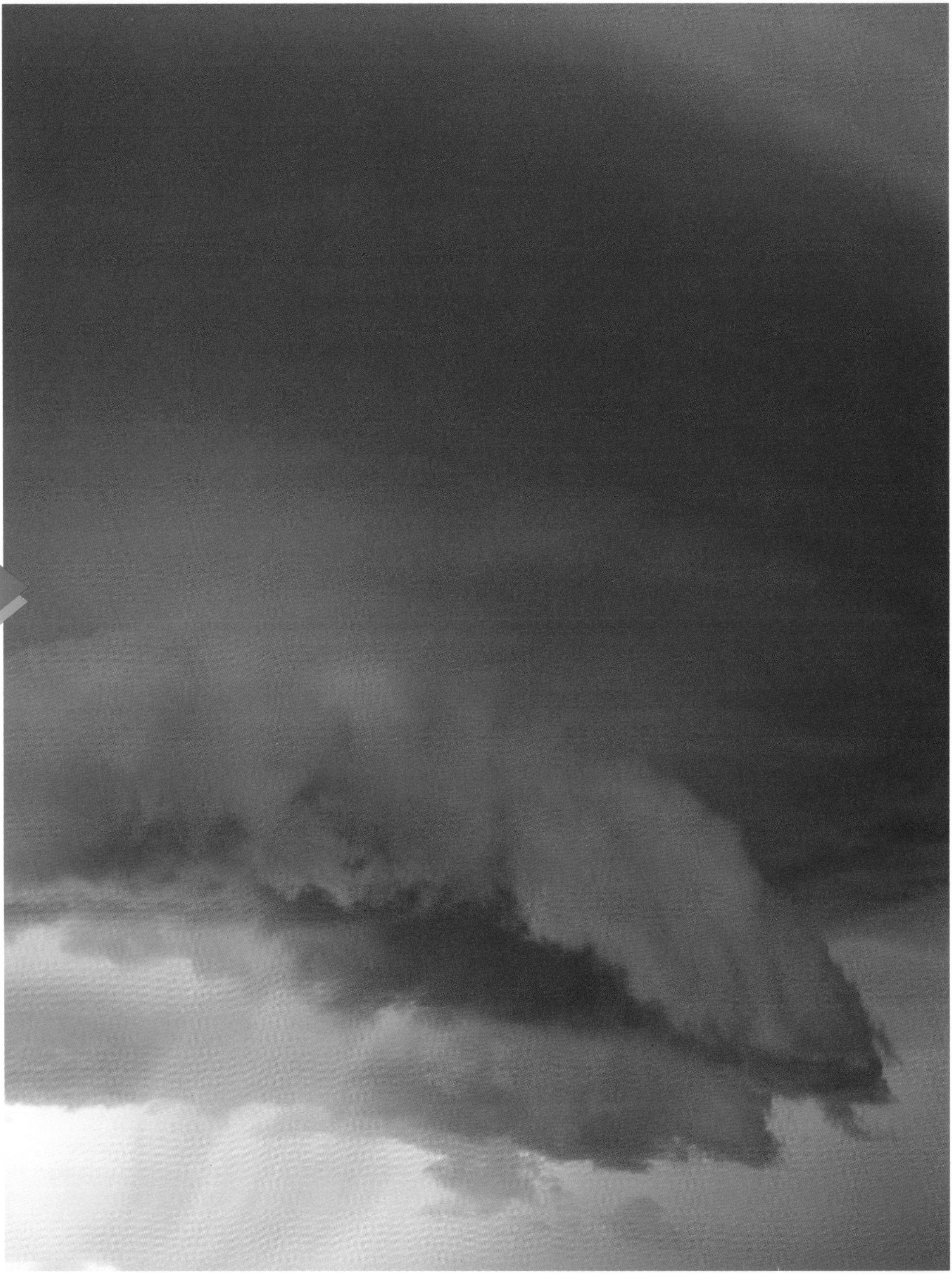

12

DIFFERENT

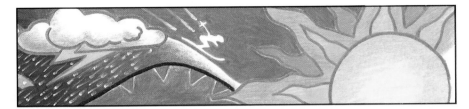

WEATHER

The surface of the Earth is curved and in some places the heat from the sun is spread out over a larger area than in other places. This means that the weather near the poles is always cold, and near the equator it is always hot. ►

◄ Prevailing winds mean that most European weather blows in from the south-west. By watching weather systems out in the Atlantic, we can predict what our weather might be a few days later.

In most parts of the world, you can expect certain weather at certain times of year. In Europe, we have four seasons—spring, summer, autumn and winter. Warmer places, such as India have only two a wet one and a dry one. ►

WEATHER AND CLIMATE

The weather in any one place changes from day to day. The climate of that place is the pattern of weather it usually has over a long period of time. At the poles the weather is always very cold, at the equator always hot and in between usually mild and damp.

▲ Polar weather is always cold even in summer.

▼ The polar, temperate and tropical parts of the world.

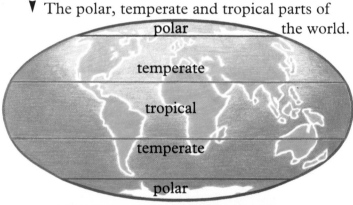

▲ In temperate parts the weather is usually warm in summer and mild and wet in winter. Mountains and places far inland have snow in winter.

Tropical areas are always very hot all through the year. Where there is plenty of rain plants grow very quickly. ►

RAINY DAYS

Huge, deep, dark cumulonimbus clouds are a sure sign of a downpour of rain. The clouds are so full of water that the sun cannot penetrate them. Lighter, thinner nimbostratus cloud gives slower, steadier rain which can last for hours or even days. Low stratus gives a misty drizzle that does not feel like rain at all. In temperate areas, it is rare for more than 4 mm of rain to fall in an hour. In tropical areas, heavy storms happen almost everyday.

Rain falls on hills when moist air cools. ▼

▲ The ground needs time to soak up heavy rain.

▲ Air is forced to rise up over hills. It cools, clouds form and rain falls on the hillside.

▲ The hillside facing away from the wind has no rain. The air has already lost most of its moisture.

WINDY DAYS

Wind is air in motion. Sometimes it is a gentle breeze, other times a fierce raging gale. Winds blow wherever there is difference in air temperature and pressure—and always from high to low pressure. By measuring the directions of the winds around the world over a long period of time, scientists have discovered huge patterns of winds that move cold air from the poles and warm air from the equator.

▲ In any one place, the wind often blows from one direction. These winds are known as prevailing winds.

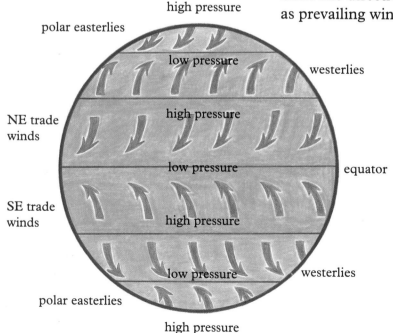

◄ Prevailing winds blow across the Earth to even up differences in pressure caused in the atmosphere by the heat of the sun. The winds blow northwards and southwards but are dragged sideways by the spinning of the Earth.

THUNDER AND LIGHTNING

Sometimes on sunny, humid days the ground heats up causing huge, towering, thunderclouds. These are heaving masses of water droplets and air in which ice crystals crash around making static electricity. Enormous electric charges build up which eventually connect to Earth in a tremendous flash of lightning. The air in the path of the flash becomes five times hotter than the surface of the sun producing a shock wave that we hear as a thunder clap.

SNOW AND ICE

When the air temperature falls below freezing, rain clouds produce snow instead of rain. If the temperature stays below freezing point all the way down to the ground then we have snow. If not, the snow turns to rain before it lands on the Earth.

▲ Snowflakes form in lacy patterns with six parts. No two snowflakes are ever the same.

In winter, snow and ice may stay for many weeks before a thaw. ▼

FROST, DEW, FOG AND MIST

When air cools, it can hold less water vapour and any extra condenses as droplets of water. In summer, dew forms on the ground at nightfall. In winter, we may wake up to find the ground sparkling with frost. Sometimes warm air is trapped under cold air. As the cold air sinks to the ground through the warmer air, fog or mist forms.

▲ On cold, clear nights there is no cloud to keep the heat in and the temperature drops sharply. Ice crystals form on trees and plants as water vapour condenses from the cold air.

◄ Fog and mist are clouds that have formed close to the ground. Warm, moist air is trapped under cold air falling from above and water droplets form.

SUNNY DAYS

Looking at the world as a whole, there are more sunny days than any other sort. Clouds are unlikely to form on sunny days because the days are probably dry and calm whereas clouds form in damp rising air. High pressure areas in which the air is gently sinking, sometimes stay in the same place for weeks on end causing long spells of sunny weather.

RAINBOWS

Each falling raindrop can act like a tiny prism. Sunlight shining on a shower of rain is bent and split into the colours of the spectrum. If the sun is low in the sky and you are standing with your back to it facing the shower of rain, you will see a rainbow in the sky.

Tropical downpours in Hawaii often cause vivid rainbows. ►

DUST IN THE AIR

When some volcanoes erupt, they eject huge amounts of fine volcanic dust. This is trapped high in the atmosphere and acts like a screen stopping some of the sun's rays reaching the Earth. Areas near the volcano suffer a drop in temperature which can last for as long as three or four years.

◄ Mount St Helens, USA, erupted in 1980 sending a huge dust cloud high into the air.

STORMS AND TORNADOES

Hurricanes and typhoons are fierce storms that start as areas of low pressure over warm sea. As they spin across the sea, they suck in heat energy and moisture growing bigger and stronger, sometimes up to 2,000 km across with winds of 300 kph. The centre of a storm is an area of dead calm with fierce gales blowing around it. When it reaches land it can no longer draw in energy from the sea so it gradually dies away.

▲ Tornadoes are fiercely whirling funnels of air in which winds can reach 500 kph. They only last about 15 minutes but suck up anything in their path. At sea, they become waterspouts.

◄ Hurricanes and typhoons cause severe damage when they reach land. Many people can be left homeless and farm crops destroyed.

WEATHER PATTERNS

The Earth formed about 4,600 million years ago but the climate has changed many times—and is still changing. There have been a number of ice-ages, when temperatures were much colder than now and huge sheets of ice covered much of the planet. Scientists around the world study weather patterns so they might understand why these changes happen.

▲ Venice at high tide. Today, scientists are worried that waste gases in the atmosphere are making the temperature of the Earth increase. They call this global warming. Just a few degrees would melt so much ice that parts of some cities like Venice, London and New York would be under water.

◄ If the world is warming up, glaciers like this one in Spitzbergen, Norway will melt.

THE SCIENCE OF

WEATHER

If you need an accurate weather forecast today, you can watch the television, listen to the radio or make a short phone call. It is only by using the most up-to-date scientific methods that these forecasts are available. ➤

◄ The science of weather watching is called meteorology. The instruments used by meteorologists range from simple thermometers and barometers to sophisticated satellite image scanners and radar.

Modern weather forecasting relies on computers to sort out all the information that comes in from thousands of weather stations around the world. This also means that the forecasts are more immediate and reliable. ➤

FRONTS, DEPRESSIONS AND LOWS

When warm air and cold air meet they don't mix very easily and a boundary called a front forms. If a kink occurs in the front, the air begins to swirl round and the pressure starts to drop. These areas are known as depressions, lows or cyclones. They travel along with a warm front in the lead and a cold front at the rear bringing rain or snow, blustery winds and lower temperatures.

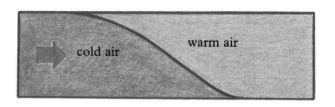

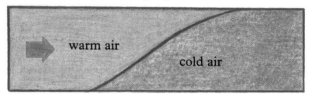

▲ A cold front forms when cold air pushes under warm air. It is drawn on a weather chart as a spiky line.

▲ A warm front forms when warm air slides up over the top of cold air. It is drawn on a weather chart as a line with bumps.

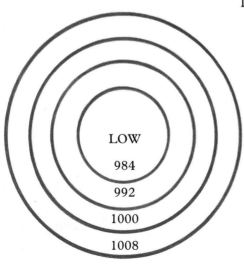

◄ Isobars are lines on a weather chart joining places which have the same pressure. The closer the lines are together the stronger the winds. Pressure is measured in millibars. Pressures above 1010 millibars are high and pressures below are low.

WEATHER CHARTS

One of the main features of any weather chart are the long, curving lines known as isobars. These lines connect all the places that have the same air pressure. Cold and warm fronts are marked around depressions and also areas of high pressure. Other symbols show wind strength and direction, cloud cover, sunshine and the likelihood of rain. Weather charts are continually revised to keep them in step with the constantly changing pattern of the weather.

KEY	
15	temperature in °C
20	wind speed

▲ The weather chart for 15 March 1993, forecast a mainly dry day for Britain.

◄ Over the Atlantic Ocean, a system of fronts and lows approaches Europe bringing rain.

GATHERING INFORMATION

The World Meteorological Organisation links 10,000 weather stations around the world which report day and night on temperature, pressure, wind speed and rainfall. Other observations are sent in from weather ships and buoys, weather balloons and aircraft.

Instruments for measuring temperature and humidity are placed inside a special box called a Stevenson screen which is open to the air but protected from rain and sun. Instruments for measuring wind and rain are placed outside. Rain is collected in a measuring bottle placed on the ground.

◄ anenometer measures the speed of the wind

weather vane measures wind direction ▼

Stevenson screen ➞

hydrograph recording changes in humidity

wet and dry thermometers measuring humidity

thermometers measuring maximum and minimum temperatures

thermograph recording changes in temperature

INFORMATION FROM SATELLITES

A number of weather satellites orbiting the Earth transmit constant information about cloud patterns and the position of weather systems. Some satellites are in orbit over the equator travelling round at the same speed as the Earth. Others circle from pole to pole photographing the Earth that spins below them. Satellite information is transmitted to ground stations which use computers to decipher it.

▲ The GOES-Next satellites to be launched during the 1990s are a new type of weather satellite. Five satellites in geostationary orbit above the equator will provide non-stop viewing of the Earth.

◄ Hurricane Bob photographed by the NOAA-11 weather satellite on 19 August 1991 as it crossed the east coast of the USA. Hurricane winds may reach speeds of 200 km per hour. NOAA satellites orbit the Earth around the poles.

FACTS ABOUT WEATHER

The windiest place on Earth is Commonwealth Bay in Antarctica where gales reach 320 km/h.

The heaviest hailstones on record weighed 1.02 kg. They fell in Bangladesh on 14 April 1986 and are said to have killed 92 people.

The highest waterspout reliably measured was seen off the coast of New South Wales, Australia in 1889. Measuring instruments on the shore gave a height of 1,528 m and a diameter of 3 m.

Some parts of the world have local winds that blow at certain times of the year changing the usual weather patterns.

Berg—hot, dry wind in South Africa.

Bora—cold and usually dry wind in NE Italy.

Buran—cold NE wind in northern Asia.

Chinook—warm, dry wind in USA.

Föhn—warm, dry wind blowing down a mountain.

Gregale—strong NE wind blowing in the Mediterranean in cooler months.

Harmattan—dry, cool wind in Africa.

Karaburan—hot, dusty wind in central Asia.

Khamsin—hot wind in Egypt in early summer.

Levanter—moist, E wind in eastern Mediterranean.

Mistral—cold, dry wind blowing down the Rhône valley in France.

Pampero—cold wind blowing across the Andes in South America.

Purga—strong NE wind in northern Asia carrying snow.

Seistan—strong N wind in Iran and Afghanistan carrying dust and sand.

Shamal—hot, dry, dusty wind in Iran and the Persian Gulf.

Sirocco—hot, dry S wind in northern Africa.

Southerly Buster—sudden strong SE wind in south eastern Australia.

Tramontana—cool, dry N wind in Spain.

Williwaw—cold, strong wind in Alaska.

Cirrus cloud is often as high as 8 km above the Earth but a very rare kind known as mother of pearl cloud sometimes forms as high as 24 km.

Sometimes very high clouds can be seen glowing in the sky long after the sun has set. These are thought to be made of dust or ice crystals about 85 km above the Earth and are known as noctilucent clouds.

St Petersburg, Florida, USA had 768 sunny days between 9 February 1967 and the 17 March 1969.

The sun shines for more than 4,000 hours on average each year at Yuma in Arizona, USA.

Desert covers about an eighth of the land surface of the Earth where the rainfall is less than 25 cm each year. The largest desert is the Sahara in Africa which covers about 8.4 million square kilometres.

It rains for up to 350 days each year on Mt Wai-'ale-'ale on the Hawaiian island of Kauai.

The temperature of a flash of lightning can reach 30,000°C which is hotter than the surface of the sun. Flashes may be as long as 30 km or as short as 100 m depending on the distance between the clouds and the Earth and can travel at speeds of up to 140,000 km/sec.

The driest place on Earth is the Atacama desert in Chile where the annual rainfall is more or less nil. For 400 years until 1971 there was no rain at all.

INDEX